BIG PICTURE SPORTS

Meet the
KANSAS CITY
CHIEFS

By
ZACK BURGESS

NORWOODHOUSE PRESS

CHICAGO, ILLINOIS

NORWOOD HOUSE PRESS

P.O. Box 316598 • Chicago, Illinois 60631
For more information about Norwood House Press please visit our website at
www.norwoodhousepress.com or call 866-565-2900.

Photo Credits:
All photos courtesy of Associated Press, except for the following: Fleer Corp. (6),
Black Book Archives (7, 15, 18), Topps, Inc. (10 both, 11 all, 22). NFL/Chiefs (23).

Cover Photo: Kevin Terrell/Associated Press

The football memorabilia photographed for this book is part of the authors' collection. The collectibles used
for artistic background purposes in this series were manufactured by many different card companies—
including Bowman, Donruss, Fleer, Leaf, O-Pee-Chee, Pacific, Panini America, Philadelphia Chewing Gum,
Pinnacle, Pro Line, Pro Set, Score, Topps, and Upper Deck—as well as several food brands, including
Crane's, Hostess, Kellogg's, McDonald's and Post.

Designer: Ron Jaffe
Series Editors: Mike Kennedy and Mark Stewart
Project Management: Black Book Partners, LLC.
Editorial Production: Lisa Walsh

LIBRARY OF CONGRESS CATALOGING-IN-PUBLICATION DATA
Names: Burgess, Zack.
Title: Meet the Kansas City Chiefs / by Zack Burgess.
Description: Chicago Illinois : Norwood House Press, [2016] | Series: Big
    picture sports | Includes bibliographical references and index.
Identifiers: LCCN 2015023949| ISBN 9781599537306 (library edition : alk.
    paper) | ISBN 9781603578332 (ebook)
Subjects: LCSH: Kansas City Chiefs (Football team)--History--Juvenile
    literature.
Classification: LCC GV956.K35 B87 2016 | DDC 796.332/6409778411--dc23
LC record available at http://lccn.loc.gov/2015023949

288N—072016
Manufactured in the United States of America in North Mankato, Minnesota

CONTENTS

Words in **bold type** are defined on page 24.

The Chiefs celebrate a touchdown.

CALL ME A CHIEF

Among Native American people, the job of chief goes to the strongest, wisest leaders. The Kansas City Chiefs take their name seriously. So do their fans. They expect the Chiefs to show strength and wisdom at all times. They know teamwork is the key to winning. That is what being a Chief is all about.

TIME MACHINE

The Chiefs played their first three seasons as the Dallas Texans. In 1963, the team moved to Kansas City, Missouri, and became the Chiefs. They joined the National Football League (NFL) in 1970. **Tony Gonzalez** ●——→ and Derrick Thomas were two of the greatest players in team history.

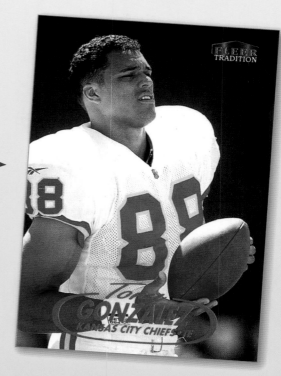

Derrick Thomas was a defensive star for the Chiefs.

Arrowhead Stadium is a fun place to watch a game.

Best Seat in the House

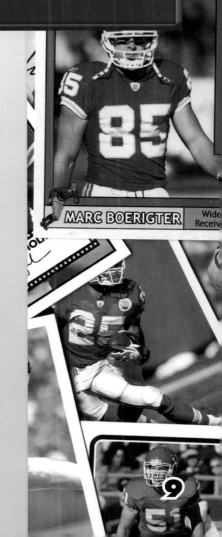

The Chiefs play in Arrowhead Stadium. It has been their home since 1972. The weather in Kansas City goes from sunny and warm in the fall to cold and wet in the winter. The players and fans are ready to win no matter what.

MARC BOERIGTER Wide Receiver

SHOE BOX

The trading cards on these pages show some of the best Chiefs ever.

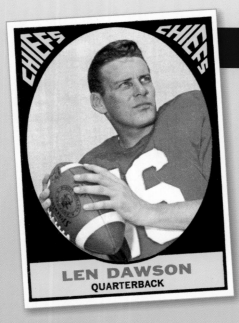

LEN DAWSON

QUARTERBACK · 1962–1975
Len was one of the smartest quarterbacks ever. He led the Chiefs to their first Super Bowl victory.

BUCK BUCHANAN

DEFENSIVE TACKLE · 1963–1975
Buck was one of the best defensive linemen of his time. He was named **All-Pro** four seasons in a row.

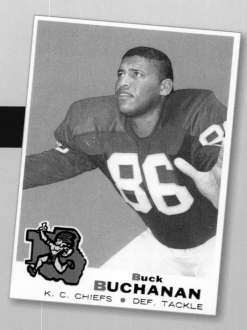

Bobby Bell

BOBBY BELL

LINEBACKER · 1963–1974

Bobby was an amazing athlete. He could have played any position on the football field.

WILLIE LANIER

LINEBACKER · 1967–1977

Willie was the first African American to play middle linebacker in the NFL. No one roamed the field with more skill or power.

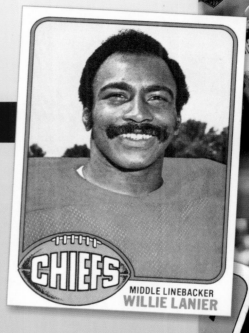

MIDDLE LINEBACKER
WILLIE LANIER

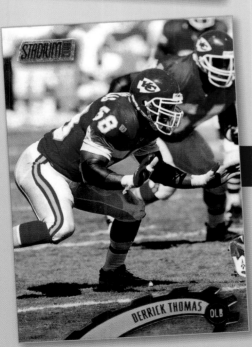

DERRICK THOMAS OLB

DERRICK THOMAS

LINEBACKER & DEFENSIVE END · 1989–1999

Derrick was almost impossible to block. He set a team record with 126.5 **quarterback sacks**.

THE BIG PICTURE

Look at the two photos on page 13. Both appear to be the same. But they are not. There are three differences. Can you spot them?

Answers on page 23.

TRUE OR FALSE?

Tony Gonzalez was a star tight end. Two of these facts about him are **TRUE**. One is **FALSE**. Do you know which is which?

1. Tony caught 102 passes in 2004.

2. Tony once put on the other team's helmet by mistake.

3. Tony made the **Pro Bowl** 10 seasons in a row for the Chiefs.

Answer on page 23.

Tony Gonzalez runs a pass pattern.

Chiefs fans go wild after a touchdown.

Go Chiefs, Go!

Chiefs fans love to wear red and make noise. In 2014, they set a world record for the loudest stadium. Before games, the parking lot of Arrowhead Stadium is a great place to eat barbecue. Fans work all week to make sure they are ready to tailgate.

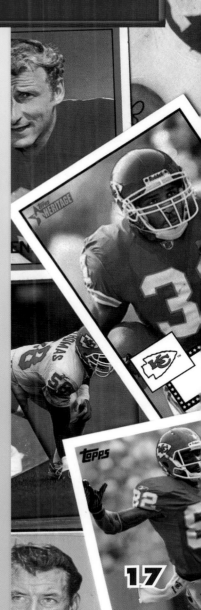

ON THE MAP

Here is a look at where five Chiefs were born, along with a fun fact about each.

 1 **MIKE GARRETT · LOS ANGELES, CALIFORNIA**
Mike's shifty running helped the Chiefs reach the Super Bowl twice.

 2 **JAMAAL CHARLES · PORT ARTHUR, TEXAS**
Jamaal was a college sprinting champion before he joined the Chiefs.

 3 **DERON CHERRY · RIVERSIDE, NEW JERSEY**
Deron was an All-Pro safety three times from 1984 to 1988.

 4 **JAN STENERUD · FETSUND, NORWAY**
Jan was one of football's best soccer-style kickers in the 1960s and 1970s.

 5 **CHRISTIAN OKOYE · ENUGU, NIGERIA**
Christian was nicknamed "The Nigerian Nightmare."

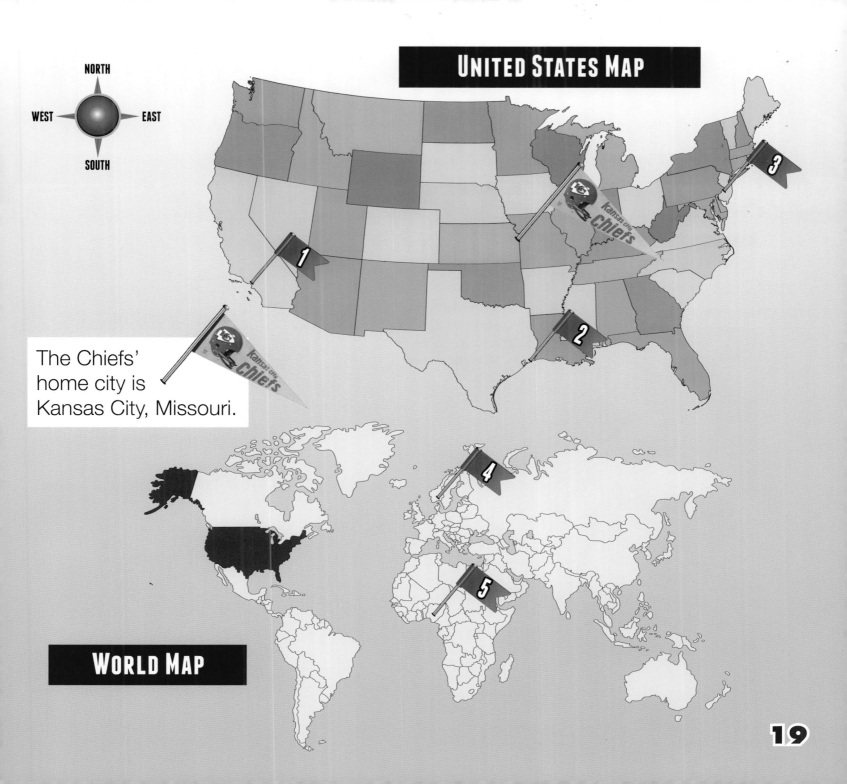

UNITED STATES MAP

NORTH
WEST — **EAST**
SOUTH

The Chiefs' home city is Kansas City, Missouri.

WORLD MAP

19

Alex Smith wears the Chiefs' home uniform.

Football teams wear different uniforms for home and away games. The Chiefs' main colors are red, gold, and white. Their uniform has barely changed since the 1960s.

Lamar Houston wears the Chiefs' away uniform.

The Chiefs' helmet is red with a white arrowhead on each side. It shows the letters *KC*. They stand for Kansas City.

WE WON!

The Chiefs won their first title in 1962 as the Dallas Texans. They were members of the **American Football League (AFL)**. The Chiefs were AFL champs again in 1967 and 1969. Those teams played great defense. Their offense relied on stars such as receiver **Otis Taylor**.

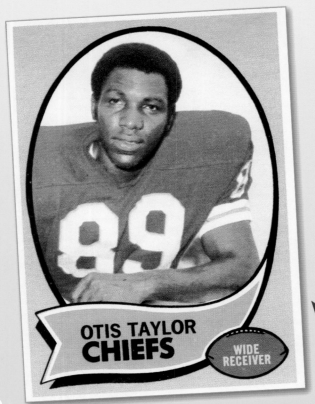

OTIS TAYLOR
CHIEFS
WIDE RECEIVER

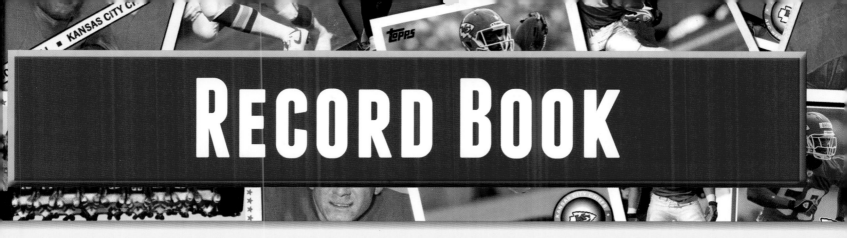

RECORD BOOK

These Chiefs set team records.

PASSING YARDS	RECORD
Season: Trent Green (2004)	4,591
Career: Len Dawson	28,507

TOUCHDOWN CATCHES	RECORD
Season: Dwayne Bowe (2010)	15
Career: Tony Gonzalez	76

POINTS	RECORD
Season: Priest Holmes (2003)	162
Career: **Nick Lowery**	1,466

ANSWERS FOR THE BIG PICTURE
#75 changed to #55, the goal posts disappeared, and the socks of the player on the far right changed to gold.

ANSWER FOR TRUE AND FALSE
#2 is false. Tony never wore the opposing team's helmet.

FOOTBALL WORDS

INDEX

All-Pro
An honor given to the best NFL player at each position.

American Football League (AFL)
A rival league of the NFL that played from 1960 to 1969.

Pro Bowl
The NFL's annual all-star game.

Quarterback Sacks
Tackles of the quarterback that lose yardage.

ABOUT THE AUTHOR

Zack Burgess has been writing about sports for more than 20 years. He has lived all over the country and interviewed lots of All-Pro football players, including Brett Favre, Eddie George, Jerome Bettis, Shannon Sharpe, and Rich Gannon. Zack was the first African American beat writer to cover Major League Baseball when he worked for the *Kansas City Star*.

ABOUT THE CHIEFS

Learn more at these websites:

www.chiefs.com • www.profootballhof.com

www.teamspiritextras.com/Overtime/html/chiefs.html